WA KĀANA HAQQAN ALAYNĀ NASRŪL MŪMINEEN

IT IS INCUMBENT UPON US TO HELP THE BELIEVERS

PREPARED AND TRANSLATED BY SHAYKH MBACKE GUEYE

All rights reserved. No part of this book may be reproduced or utilized in any form or by any means, electronic or mechanical, including photocopying, recording, or by any information storage or retrieval system, without permission in writing from the publisher, except as provided by U.S.A. copyright law.

Djannatul Mahwa Publishing
Copyright © November 11, 2021, by Shiloh Lamp Fall
Printed in the United States of America

WA KĀANA HAQQAN ALAYNĀ NASRŪL MŪMINEEN

COMPOSITION

Wa Kāana Hàqqan Alaynā Nasrul Mūmineen was composed in 1323 Hijrī during the exile of the Shaykh Ahmadou Bamba in Mauritania during the holy month of Ramadan i.e. a year after he received the Wird al Makhūz from the Prophet Muhammad (saws). Its metric is Rajaz and it is a qasīda of supplication (dua), confidence with Allah (munājāt), praises (hamd), and an expression of gratitude (shukr). This is an amazing qasīda written after the exile of the Shaykh in Gabon and He said regarding this category that they are higher in privileges and rank than any good deeds apart from the Quran and hadiths of the Prophet (saws). It is a compilation of three acrostics:

1. The last part of verse 47 of Surah 30 (Ar-Rum) in the Holy Quran namely "...*and it is incumbent upon Us to help the believers*".

   Walaqad arsalna min qablika rusulane ilaa qawmihim fajaoohum bilbayyinati fantaqamna minal-latheena ajramoo Wa Kaana haqqan AAalayna nasrul mumineena

   [And certainly We sent before you messengers to their people, so they came to them with clear arguments, then We gave the punishment to those who were guilty; and it is incumbent upon Us to help the believers.]

   This is the Ayah (Surah 40:37) which the qasīda is named after; it is composed of 24 letters in which the Shaykh repeated the ayah 3 times to make it **72 verses**.

2. The beginning of verse 195 of Surah 3 (Āl Imrān) in the Holy Quran namely "*fastajāba lahum Rabbuhum*". This Ayah (Surah 3:195) is composed of 15 letters in which the Shaykh reiterated twice to make it **30 verses**.

Fastajaba lahum rabbuhum annee la odeeAAu AAamala AAamilin minkum minthakarin aw ontha baAAdukum min baAAdinfallatheena hajaroo waokhrijoo min diyarihimwaoothoo fee sabeelee waqataloo waqutiloolaokaffiranna AAanhum sayyi-atihim walaodkhilannahum jannatintajree min tahtiha al-anharu thawabanmin AAindi Allahi wallahu AAindahu husnuaththawab

[So their Lord accepted their prayer: That I will not waste the work of a worker among you, whether male or female, the one of you being from the other; they, therefore, who fled and were turned out of their homes and persecuted in My way and who fought and were slain, I will most certainly cover their evil deeds, and I will most certainly make them enter gardens beneath which rivers flow; a reward from Allah, and with Allah is yet better reward.]

3. The last acrostic of this qasīda is "*And no soul knows what has been hidden for them of comfort for eyes as reward for what they used to do.*" This Ayah (Surah 32:17) was used to write make **48 verses**, the numerical value of Hā Mīm, that is to say altogether the qasīda is composed of **150 verses**.

falā ta'lamu nafsun mā ukh'fiya lahum min qurrati a'yunin jazāan bimā kānū ya'malūn

So no soul knows what is hidden for them of that which will refresh the eyes; a reward for what they did.

Context

Abdullah ibn Ay-ēh a Banî Daymān a Mauritanian cleric and very knowledgeable man dreamed about the Shaykh composing an acrostic with the Ayah (Wa Kāana Hàqqan Alaynā Nasrul Mūmineen) upon his request when he woke up, he then informed the Shaykh and the latter went into his room to grab the qasīda freshly written according to Shaykh Muhammad al Bashīr in Minanul Bāqil Qadīm (Gifts of the Everlasting). Some verses in the qasīda emphasize that thesis such as:

Wajih li ummati rassūli lāhi, alayhi khayrou salawati lahi...

Give victory to the nation of the Prophet Muhammad may Allah's blessings be upon him...

Nājaytukal yawma bi hamdin wa chukūr, fil mumineena. Yaa Waliyyu yaa Chakūr

I communicated with you today praise and gratitude for all believers. O you the Guardian, the Grateful

SPECIFICITY

In this book, Shaykh Ahmadou Bamba shows true tawheed and gratefulness to Allah (*Azza wa Jal*) in the first verse in which he says: *"I surrender myself entirely with praise and thanks, to the Protecting Friend of the Believers, the Grateful One"*. His love (Mahabbah) for the Prophet (saws) and mastery of the Arabic language made it mandatory, to explain what is necessary and is not necessary for poetry (*luzūmu mā lā yalzam*). This book is a source of joy full of benefits and virtues for believing men and women.

BENEFITS AND VIRTUES

- ⇒ Each of the letters is a source of pleasure for Allah (*Azza wa Jal*) and the Prophet (PBUH)
- ⇒ Every letter brings joy to the hearts of the believers, male and female
- ⇒ The one that reads this qasīda will have their needs satisfied beyond their expectations.
- ⇒ The qasīda is protection against fitnah (e.g. temptation, trial, sedition, civil strife or conflict)[1]
- ⇒ This writing is a protection against non-believers (infidels) and non-muhsins
- ⇒ This composition is a protective shield against Shirk (ascribing partners to Allah) and hypocrisy.

The benefits and privileges of the qasīda are too many to be numbered, so we have just picked a few of them to share particularly those who do not know much about this qasāid of Shaykh Al Khadim. May Allah accept our khidma (sacrificial Service) by the blessings of **Wa Kāana Hàqqan `Alaynā Nasrul Mūmineen.**

Written by Mouhamadou Bao
Edited by Yahya abd al Alim Coats

---

[1] Fitnah comes from the word fa-ta-na which means to seduce, enchant and captivate. It is found several times in the Quran; used with a negative connotation.

PREAMBLE

I seek refuge in Allah from Satan the accursed, and I do seek protection in Allah from his offspring, Lord preserve me from the whispering of the Devil. I seek protection from thee lest they are present before me. Ô Allah by the sanctity of your face! O you the Generous send your prayers and peace upon our master Muhammad, his family, and companions. Ô You who have approved these letters, and made it rejoiceful to your Prophet (pbuh), and bliss to every believer male or female, Ameen. Ô thou who said, **"Wa Kāana Hàqqan `Alaynā Nasrul Mūmineen"**.

WA KĀANA HAQQAN ALAYNĀ NASRŪL MŪMINEEN
(IT IS INCUMBENT UPON US TO HELP THE BELIEVERS)

BISMILLAH IR RAHMAN IR RAHEEM
IN THE NAME OF ALLAH, MOST GRACIOUS, MOST MERCIFUL

وجّهت كلّي بحمد وشكور
إلى وليّ المؤمنين والشّكور

Wajjahhtu kuliya bi hamdine wa-chukûr
Ila waliyyi-l-mu'minina wa-chakûr

I surrender myself entirely with praise and thanks, to the Protecting Friend of the Believers, the Grateful One.

كن يا وليّ يا قدير يا نصير
للمؤمنين إنّك الهادي البصير

Kun yā waliyyu yâ qadîru yâ nasîr
Li'l mu'minina innaka-l- hâdi-l- basīr

O Holy One! O Almighty, O Helper, be with the believers for you are the guide and the seer

أذهبت فورا لسوانا كلّ من
ليس يكون مومنا يا ذا الزّمن

Az habta fawrane lisiwana kulla man
Laysa yakûna mūminane yaaza zaman

You immediately drove away from me anyone who disbelieves, O You Owner of Times

أذهبت فورا لسوانا كلّ من
ليس يكون مسلما يا ذا الزّمن

Az habta fawrane lisiwana kulla man
Laysa yakûna musliman yaza zaman

You immediately drove away from me anyone who does not submit to Islam

أذهبت فورا لسوانا كلّ من
ليس يكون محسنا يا ذا الزمن

Az habta fawrane lisiwana kulla man
Laysa yakûna muhsinan yaza zaman

You have immediately turned away from me anyone who lacks spiritual perfection

نفعتنا به وبالإيمان
فالتنفع الجميع بالأمان

Nafa'tanâ bi-afdali- l- Imâni
Fal tanfa'il jami'a bil amâni

You have been helpful to them by granting them a superior faith, being useful to all by providing them with security

حفظتهم به وبالإسلام
فالتنفع الكلّ عن الملام

Hafiztahum bi-hî wabil islâmi
Fal tahfasil Kulla anil malâmi

Through faith and Islam, you have protected them. So watch over them and protect them from blame.

قدّمت سيّد البرايا أحمدا
والأنبيا والرّسل يا من حمدا

Qad-damta sayyidal barayaa Ahmada
Wal Anbiyya wa- rusli yâ man houmida

O You the Praised One, You have given precedence to the Master of Mankind, Prophets, and the Angels (Muhammad)

قد الصّلاة والسّلام أبدا
لهم كما أخزيت من لم يعبدا

Qoudis-salâta wa salama abada
Lahoum kamâ akhzayta man lam ya'bouda

Grant them always blessings and salvation contrary to how You covered with shame those that do not worship You

إلى النّبي قد الصّلاة والسّلام
والأنبيا والرّسل منزل الكلام

Ilan Nabi quids Salata was salam
Wal Anbiya war Rousil mounzilal kalam

You who revealed the word, grant blessing to the Prophet and the other messengers and apostles

علي النّبي محمّد والآل
صلّ وسلّم واستجب سؤالي

**Alan Nabi Muhamadin wall aali
Salli wa Salim wastajib sou-âli**

To the Prophet Muhammad and his followers, grant blessings and greetings and grant my request

للمنتقى اكتب ما يسرّه بلا
نهاية وخدمتي تقبّلا

**Lil Mountaqa- ouktoub maa yasurruhou bila
Nihayatin wa kidmatî taqabbalâ**

Decree without end what makes the Chosen One happy, accept my service

يسّر لسيّد الورى مااختارا
يا باقيا جعله مختارا

**Yassir li sayidi-l- warâ makhtârâ
Ya bâqiyan ja'alahou moukhtârâ**

Facilitate for the Master of Mankind (Muhammad) all of his desires, O You the Everlasting who has made him the chosen by excellence

نافع صلّ والتسلّم في أبد
علي اللّذي لك يقود من عبد

**Nâfi-u salli wal tusalim fi abad
Alalazy lakka yaqudu man abad**

O Useful One, grant Your prayer and Your salvation eternally to him who leads to You every worshipper

أكتب صلاة لجميع الأنبيا
والرّسل بالتّسليم واشكر كتبيا

Uktub salatane li djamihil-anbiyâ
War-rusli bit taslîmi wachkur kutbiya

Send prayers to all the prophets as well as the envoys with a greeting and approve my writings

نافع صلّ والتسلّم باالاحترام
علي النبي والآل والصّحب الكرام

Nafi'u sale wal tusalim bihtiram
Alan Nabî wall âli was Sahbil kiram

O Useful One, grant blessing, salvation, and respect to the Prophet, his family, and his noble companions

صلاة ذي العرش العظيم الصّمد
علي النّبي وآله والحمّد

Salâtou zil'archil'azîmi Samadi
Alan Nabi wa alihi wal hum'madi

May the blessing of the Master of the Immense Throne, the Eternal One, be granted upon Muhammad (pbuh) and to those who praise Allah consistently.

ردّ مكائد العدي إلي العدي
يا من حباني بمخجل عدي

Rudda makâ-idaa ilal idaa
Yâ man habaniya bi moukhjili idâ

Turn the evil plans of the enemies to the enemies, O You who gave me that which enables me to confound my enemies

أوصل لكلّ مسلم ومسلمة
مسرّة يا من كفاني ظلمة

**Awsil likoulli mouslimine wa Muslima
Masaratan yâ man kafaani zalama**

Grant felicity to every muslim, men and women, Ô You who protected me from the offenders

لكلّ مومن وكلّ مومنة
أوصل بشارات لصفو مدمنة

**Li kulli mou'minine wa kulli mou-mina
Awsil bouchâratine Lisafwine mudminah**

Grant your everlasting happiness to every believing man and believing woman

مدّ لكلّ محسن ومحسنة
أعلي بشارات تري مستحسنّة

**Mudda likoulli mouhsinine wa mouhsina
A'la bouchratine tourā moustahsana**

To every benefactor and every benefactress grant the greatest joys that can be enjoyed!

وجّه لأمّة رسول الله
عليه خير صلواة الله

**Wajjihi li umma'ti rasoulil lâhi
Alayhi khayrou salawâtil lâhi**

Turn to the community of Allah's apostle, may the best of divine blessings be bestowed upon him

مدد من متي يقل كن يكن
يا من يكوّن مني لم تكن

Mada da man matā yaqul koun yakuni
Yâ man youkawinou mu'nane lam takuni

The succor (help) of Him (Allah) whom whenever He says to a thing be it is. Ô You who conceives wishes that do not exist

ناجيتك اليوم بحمد وشكور
في المومنين يا وليّ يا شكور

Nâjaytoukal yawma bi hamdine wa chukur
Fil mouminîna yâ waliyyou yâ chakūr

I communicated with You today giving You thanks and praise for the believers, O Grateful One

يقود لي كن فيكون حاجي
منك بلا حقد ولا تحاج

Yaqudu li koune fa yakounou hâji
Minka Bila hiqdine walâ tahâji

You have granted me the power (Kun) to do whatever I desire without hatred or argument

نفيت إبليس لغيري أبدا
في شهر ذا وكلّ من لم يعبدا

Nafayta Iblisa li ghayri Abada
Fi-chahri za wa koulla man lam ya'bouda

In this month (Ramadan) You chased away Iblis [away from me] forever as well as those that do not worship You

وجّه لمن قد آمنوا وأسلموا
وأحسنوا مخجل من لم يسلموا

Wajih liman qad âmanû wa aslamū
Wa ahsanû moukhjila man lam youslimū

Direct to those who have believed, performed their religious duties accordingly, and perfected their spirits, what non-believers will always envy them for

كوّن لأمّة النّبي صلّا
عليه بالتّسليم ربّ جلّا

Kawin li um'mati Nabiyyi sallâ
Alayhi bî Taslimi Rabbun Jallaa

Grant the same favor to the community of the Prophet, upon him be the salutation of the Majestic Lord

إجابة تزحزح الأعدائنا
إلى سواهم سرمدا ودائنا

Ijabatan touzahzihoul ahda-a
Ila siwahoum abdane wadda-â

A favorable answer that drives away from them, enemies and plagues towards others!

نافع يا كريم يا مهيمن
لي استجب وللّذي يهيمن

Nâfi'u yâ karîmou yâ Mouhayminou
Liyas-tadjib wali -l- lazī youhayminou

O Useful One, O Generous One, O Guardian by excellence! Answer me favorably and everyone who says, Ameen

حفيظ صن أمّة خير مرسل
عن اللّذين كفروا بالرّسل

**Hafizu sun ummata khayri Mursali
Anil lazîna kafarû bî roussouli**

O You, the Guardian by excellence! Keep the community of the Best Apostle away from those who disbelieved the Messengers

قد لهم نصرا عزيزا آجلا
وبشّرنهم عاجلا وآجلا

**Qud lahoumou nasrane'Azizane ajilá
Wa bachiranhoum âjilan wa ajilâ**

Give them a bright victory in this world! Give them the good news in this world and the hereafter

قد لزوي الإيمان ما يزيد
حبّك يا من عنده مزيد

**Qud li dhawil imâni ma Yazidu
Houbaka yâ man indahu mazidu**

Give to the followers of Islam that which increases Your Love to them O You, who increases!

أغن ذوي الإسلام عن ركون
إلي عداك وعن السّكون

**Aghni dhawil Islami an rukūni
Ilâ idāka wa ani soukûni**

Exempt those who have faith from the constraint of having to rely on Your enemies or having to depend on them

علي النّبيّ والرّسول الملتحد
صلّ وسلّم يا مبيد من جحد

Ala Nabiyyi wa-rasoulil multahad
Salli wa Salim yâ mubida man jahad

To the Prophet, the Apostle, grant blessing and salvation, O You who exterminates the negators

للمنتقى والآل والصّحب الكرام
أوصل سلاميك وجد لي بالمرام

Lil Mountaqâ wall âli wa-Sahbil kirâm
Awsil salâmayka wa jud li bil marâm

To the Chosen One, his family, and his noble companions grant blessing and salvation and grant my wishes

ياسن له الخلق كما له الأسور
يا مغنيا أغنيتني عن الضّمير

Yâ man lahul khalqu kamā Lahu umūr
Yâ mughniyane aghnaytanî 'ani damir

O You, Owner of all Création and all things, O You who are Sufficient, who has saved me from slander

ناجيتك اليوم وأمس راجيا
ولي قديت دون شكّ حاجيا

Nâ jaytukal yawma wa amsi râjiyâ
Wa li qadayta dûna chakkin hâjiya

I have spoken to You today (present) and yesterday (past). And without a doubt, You have satisfied my needs

أوصل لأمّة النّبي أحمدا
مصلّيا عليه في من حمدا

Awsil li ummatin nabiyyi Ahmadá
Mousaliyan 'Alayhi fîman humida

Grant to the community of Prophet Muhammad (pbuh), upon him be prayers from amongst the praised ones

نصرا عزيزا يشمل الكبارا
مع الصّغار رض لهم من بارا

Nasran azizan yachmouloul kibârâ
Ma'ha sighari roudh lahoum man bara

A dazzling victory for the great (elderly) as well as the little ones (youth)! Help them vanquish their contenders

صن الحديث والفروع كالكتاب
عن اللّذين امتنعوا من المتاب

Sounil haditha walfouru'a kal kitab
Anil lazeenam tanaū minal matâb

Safeguard the hadith, it's branches [of sciences] as well as the book (Quran) from those who refuse to repent

رافع بي ارفع الكتاب والفرروع
مع الأحاديث الصّحاح ذا بروع

Râfihou bi irfahil kitaba wal furuh
Mahal ahaadis assihâhi za buruh

Oh You, the Excellent, elevate me with the book, the science of theology, and the authentic hadith with eloquence

أعطيتني الجميع دون سلب
ولي تقود السّوَل وقت الطّلب

Ahtaytani – l – jami'a dûna sala bi
Wali taqûdus su-la waqta talabi

You have given me everything without taking it away from me! You have fulfilled my wish just as I was making it

لي أوصل اللّذي أريد وانفع
بي الوري يا مغنيا عن مدفع

Li awsalil lazy our idol wanfa'i
Biyal wara yâ Loughnan an midfa'i

Grant me what I want! Make me useful to humanity! O You who protected me from cannons

محوت قصد الضّرّ لي بالمنتقي
وقدت لي ما ودّه ذوو النّقي

Mahawta qasda dhurri lî bil Mountaqa
Wa qudta li ma waddahū dhawut tuqa

You have turned away the arrows of evil from me through the grace of the Chosen One by excellence and You have granted me what the righteous people desired

وجّهت لي ما لا يزال عجبا
في أبد للصّالحين النّجبا

Wajjahta li mâ là yazâlu 'ajaba
Fi abadine lissâlikhîna nujaba

You have given me that which will never cease to be the object of wonder in the eyes of the righteous saints

مددت لي مدد من لا يخفي
عليه شيء جدت لي بالأخفي

Madadta li madada man lê yakhfâ
Alayhi chayun judta lī bil akhfâ

You have granted me graces Oh, you whom nothing escapes.
And You have been generous to me, You imparted me hidden secrets

نفيّت كلّ من قلاني فهرب
لما يسوئه دواما ذا كرب

Nafayta kulla man qalânî faharab
Lî mâ yasû-uhû dawâman zâ kurab

You have driven away from me anyone who has hated me by making him flee, toward evil that will eternally make him distressed

يا الله يا رحمان يا بصير
قادر يا رحيم يا نصير

Yal lāhou yâ Rahmânu yâ Bassirū
Qâdiru yà Rahîmu yâ Nassiru

Oh Allah! Oh Clement! Oh Clairvoyant!
Oh Mighty One! Oh Merciful One! Oh Helper!

نجّيت من بي تعلّقوا معا
من الشّياطين فشكري اسمعا

Najayta man Biya ta'allaqû mahā
Mina chayâtîni fa chukriyas-ma'hâ

You have saved those who are attached to me from Devils (men and djinn). So accept my gratitude!

وجّهت شكري إلي الرّحمان
المالك الرّحيم ذي الأزمان

Wajahtu chukriya ila Rahmâni
Al mâliki Rahîmi zil azmâni

I address my gratitude to the Clement, the King and the Merciful Owner of Time

كرّمني في موضعي وبلدي
مكرّم بالأمن صفًا خلدي

Karramanî fî mawdihî wa baladi
Mukarrimun bil amni saffâ khaladī

The Generous One has honored me in my land, [more] precisely in my abode (Holy City of Touba). He has made my stay enjoyable and secure

أكرمني الرّحمان إكراما كفي
كليتي الضّر وفيضي وكفا

Akramani Rahmânou ikrâman kafâ
Kulliyatid dhurrie wa faydi wakafā

The Clement has honored me in a way that has completely warded off all evils and my mystical graces have flowed in abundance

ناجيت ربّي بشهر رمضان
شهر الأمان والمنى والفيضان

Nâjaytu rabiya bi chahri Ramadan
Chahril amani wall mounâ wal fayadān

I have addressed my Lord in the month of Ramadan, the month of safety, hope, and graces

حمدته حمدا يسوق سرمدا
لغيرنا إبليس سوقا أكمدا

Hamidtuhû Hamdan yasûqu sarmada
Lighayrinâ Iblissa chawqane akmada

My praises to Allah will forever drive away Iblis (the devil) from me, and he is in constant grief

قلوب جملت العدي توجّهت
لغير ضرّي والمنى لي وجّهت

Qulûbu jumlatil 'idâ tawaj-jahate
Li ghayri durri wal mounâ lee wuj-jihate

The hearts of all enemies have been tamed so as not to harm me, and all blessings are headed forward

قلوب جملة اللّذين أفلحوا
لي توجّهت وربّي المصلح

Qulûbu jumlatil lazeena aflahū
Liya tawaj-hate wa rabbil muslihu

The hearts of those who will be happy are directed to me and my Lord is the Reformer

إلى اللّذين ظلموني قبل
نحت مضرّتي كذاك الكبل

Ila lazina zalamūnî qablū
Nahat madar-ratī kaza kal kablu

Against those who had unjustly persecuted me, the harm and tribulations have returned to them

عنّي انتفت مضرّتي والبلوي
بفضل مغن لي قاد الحلوي

Annin-tafat maddarratī wal balwa
Bifadhli mughnine Liya qâdal hulwa

The persecution and the trials are over for me, [thanks] to the goodness of the One who is sufficient for me and who has afterward given me a sweet existence

له شكوري إلي الجنّات
دار المني والأمن والمنّات

Lahû chuukûriya ill jannati
Dâril munâ wall amnî wal-minâti

Consequently, I will thank Him until Paradise, the abode of supreme aspirations, security, and blessings

يشكره كلّي بالكتاب
بلا معادات ولا عتاب

Yachkuruhû kulliya bil kitâbi
Bilâ mu'adatine wa là 'itâbi

I am grateful to Him with my entirety and through the Holy Book
Without quarrels or reproaches

ناجيته تناجي التّكريم
ولم يزل بنافع كريم

Na jaytuhū tanādjya -at -Takrimi
Wa lam yaazal bi nâfi'ine Karimi

I communicated with Him with all honors, and He never ceases to be helpful and generous

إليه وجّهت هنا خطابا
مع اليقين وفؤادي طابا

Ilayhi wajjahtu hunâ khitâbâ
Mahal yaqini wa fu-âdî tâbâ

I address Him this communication with certainty and my heart is quieted

نصرتني فإنّك النّصير
محوت عيبي إنّك البصير

Nasaratani fa-innakan nassiru
Mahawta aybi innakal bassîru

You have helped me; You are the Helper. You have erased my vice; You are the All-Seeing

صمد قد أوصلت لي في رمضان
ما رمت منك قبله بفيضان

Samadu qad awsaltali fi Ramadan
Mâ rumtu Minka qablahû bi fayadân

Lord, You have granted me in the month of Ramadan, with abundance what I wished to obtain from You before

رددت لي فيه اللّذي أحببتا
لي وجالب الأذي ذببتا

Radadta li fihi lazy ahbabtâ
Liya wa jâlibal azâ zababtâ

You have given me back what I wanted and You have removed all sources of persecution from me

أجبتني جواب من تعالي
عن سنة وقدت لي انفعالا

Ajabtani djawaba man ta'âlâ
An sinnatine wa qudta li-n-fi'âlâ

You have given me a favorable answer, Oh You who are too high to fall asleep And You have made this answer concrete

لوجهك الكريم أوصل فرجا
للمومنين والتحقّق الرّجا

Li wadjhikal karîmi awsil Farajaa
Lil mouminina wall tuhaqiqir-rajā

For the sake of Your Generous Face, bring joy to the believers and fulfill their hope

مصلّيا مسلّما علي النّبي
بشير كلّ أقرب وأجنب

Mousalliyan mousalliman Hala Nabi
Bachirī kulli aqrabin wa ajnabi

Granting blessings and peace to the Prophet, the bearer of the good news for anyone who lives near or far

وليّ هب للمسلمين فرحه
يا من محي عنّي الأذي وترحه

Waliyyu hab Lil mouslimîna furha
Yâ man mahâ hanil aza wat tarha

O Guardian, grant joy to the Muslims! O you who has removed persecution and sorrow from me

محوت ما عليّ مرّ من بلا
يا من جميع خدمي تقبّلا

Mahawta mā alayya marra min balâ
Yâ man jamaiha khidamî taqabbalah

You have removed all the hardships that I have gone through You who accepted all my services

نجّ عيال المصطفى بعد صلاة
مع سلام من عداهم القلاة

Naji hiyâlal Mustapha bahda salah
Ma'a salâmin man hidâhumul qulah

After granting blessings and salvation, save the family of the Chosen One [from the clutches] of their hateful enemies

يسّر لهم به اللّذي تعسّرا
فكلّ ما يسّرته تيسّرا

Yassir lahum bihil lazy ta 'assarà
Fakullu mâ yassartahû tayassara

For the sake of the Prophet, smooth out all their difficulties, for whatever You make easy shall be

ناجاك عبدك خديم عبدك
مرتجيا نيل المنى من عندكا

Nâjâka 'abduka khadimu abdika
Mourtajiyan naylal mûna min 'Indika

Your slave and the Privileged Servant of Your slave (Muhammad, the Prophet) had just communicated with You hoping to obtain the fulfillment of his wishes from You

فاز اللّذين سعدوا بالخير
وباء من لم يسعدوا بضير

Fazal lazīna sahidû bil Khayri
Wa bâ-a man lam yas 'adû bi dayri

Happy are the ones who have obtained the good, the unfortunate ones are those who have fallen into damnation

أكرمة الأبرار بالنّعيم
وكبّت الفجّار في الجحيم

Ukrimatil abráru bin nahîmi
Wa kubbatil fujjâru fil Jahīmi

The blessed ones are honored in Paradise, and the ungodly are overthrown in Hell

سيق اللّذين تركوا العباده
لنار من من لم يتب أباده

Sikha lazīna tarakûl 'ibada
Linâri man lam youtih abada

Those who abandon the worship of Allah will be cast in the Hellfire of the One, who annihilates whoever disobeys Him

تعب من أراد أن ينقد ما
أبرمه من ضيفه لم يدما

Tahîba man arada an yanquda mâ
Abrâmahû mane dayfuhú lame yudama

Whoever wants to destroy what has been built by Allah only fatigues himself. It is Him whose host is not persecuted.

جزاء من بارز ذا العرش بكا
فكلّ من أبكاه ذو الكرسي بكا

Jazâ-u man bâraza zal archi buka
Fakullu man abkâhu zul'koursî baka

The wages of anyone who measures himself against the Master of the Throne will be in tears. For every being whom, He makes weep, shall weep

إنّ اللّذين كفروا وامتنعوا
من توبة رؤوا جزا ما صنعوا

Innal lazīna kafarû wam tana'u
Min tawbatin ra-aw jazâ mâ Sana'u

The non-believers who refuse to repent will see the price of their deeds

بطونهم سكنها العقارب
والكلّ منهم من صديد شارب

Butûnuhum sakanahal'aqâribu
Wal Kullu minhum min sadīdine châribu

Their bellies will be inhabited by scorpions and each of them will drink from a source of pus (boiling water)

للمسلمين ولكلّ المسلمات
نور اللّذي أذهب أهل الظّلمات

Lil muslimīna wa li kullil muslimât
Nûru ladhî adhaba Ahlu zulumât

May the light of Him who banished the people of darkness be upon every Muslim man and woman

هم اللّذين في الجنان يخلدون
وهم بما يسرّهم مخلّدون

Humul lazīna fil jinâni yakhludûn
Wahum bimâ yassurruhum mukhlladūn

These are the chosen ones who dwell eternally in Paradise, and they will experience eternal happiness

مناهم احتووا بلا استلاب
والكلّ بالبشر ذو انقلاب

Munāhumuh tawaw Bila-n- silābi
Walkullu bil bucharri zunqilabi

They see all their wishes come true, they will not lose their bliss. And all will bask in joy

رجائهم محقّقن وملكوا
في أبد ما لا يراه ملك

Raja - uhum mahaqqqun wa muliku
Fi abadine mâ lâ yarâhu maliku

Their hope has been fulfilled and they possess furthermore what a king has never enjoyed

بنائهم يعلو وليس ينسفل
أمّا مبارز العلي فمنسفل

Binâ uhum yahlu wa laytha yansafil
Ammâ mubarizul'alî fa munfasil

Their building will be elevated and will not be lowered, but the enemy of the Highest will be always downgraded

بالله آمنوا وأسلموا معا
والتحسنوا لوجه باق قمعا

Billâhi âminû wa aslimû ma'hâ
Waltuhsinû liwajhi bâqin qamaha

I recommend that you have faith in Allah and be Muslims all of you, act appropriately for the sake of the Eternal One, the Subduer

هو الأله وهو الرّحمان
وهو الرّحيم وله الأزمان

Huwal llâhu wah war-Rahmânu
Wahwa- Rahimu wa lahul Azmânu

He is Allah. And He is the Merciful, and to Him belongs the times

منّي له أنفع حمد وشكور
ذا خدمت للمصطفى عبد الشّكور

Mini lahû anfa'u hamdin wa chukar
Zâ Kjidmatin Lil Mustaphâl'abdich chakûr

May He receive from me the warmest thanks and the most exalted praise I do in my ability as a servant of the Chosen One, the grateful slave

فارقت جملة مز المباح
لمن كفاني ذوي النّباح

Fāraqtu jumlatan minal mubahi
Liman kafâniya zawî nûbâhi

I renounced a set of permissible things for the sake of the one who protected me against the evil of the owners of barking dogs (i.e. French Colonialist)

أشكره وقاد لي أبدالا
كما كفاني الحرب والجدالا

Ashkuruho wa qada lî abdaláa
Kama kafânîl harba wall jidâlâ

I am grateful to Him as He has given me alternatives (in exchange for what He had renounced) and has safeguarded me from war and disputes (controversy)

سبحانه وهو الكريم والحميد
فكلّ من لم يحوني فهو كميد

Subhanahû wahwal Karimi wal Hamid
Wa Kullu man lam yahwanî fahwa kamid

Glory be to Him, the Noble One, the Worthy of Praise, and whoever does not love me will experience sorrow

تسليم من لي لا يوجّه الضّرر
علي اللّذي به كفاني الغرر

Taslimu man lilâ yuwajjihu darar
All lazî bihî kafâniyal gharar

May the peace of Him, who never allows harm to come near me, be upon him, through whom Allah has protected me from illusions

جزاء من جلّ عن المثال
لي قاد ما غاب عنةالأمثال

Jazâ-u man jalla 'anil mithâli
Li gâda mâ ghāba 'anil amthâli

I have received the salary of the One who has no equal, who has granted me that which my likeness does not have

الحمد لله بلا انتهاء
علي ابن عبد الله ذي البهاء

Alhamdu lillâhi bilan that-i
Albini habdillâhi zil bahâ-i

Praise be to Allah without end for giving us the son of Abdullah, the magnificent

براعة المختار ليست تخفي
إلاّ علي من بنكال يخفي

Barrà Atul Mukhtari laysat taxfa
Illà 'allà man bi nakalin yukhfâ

The excellence of the Chosen One is hidden from those whom damnation covers with darkness

للمصطفي وجّهت ما قد صرفا
لغيرنا إبليس وهو انصرفا

Lil Mustaphâ wafjahtu mâ qad sarafa
Lighayrina Iblissa wahwan sarafaa

By the grace of Al Mustapha (Chosen One), I turned away elsewhere, [from] the evil that Iblis sought to bring to me

هدمت باطلا بحقّ فزحق
ولي إلاهي كأس سقيه دهق

Haddamtu bâtilan bihaqqin fa zahaq
Wali illâhi ka-sa saqyihî dahaq

I have thrown down the edifice of falsehood with the truth, the lie has vanished, and Allah has filled my cup with a sweet drink

ملّكت ربّي مالكي كلّيتي
حالي له كعملي ونيّتي

Mallaktu rabbî mâlikî kulliyatti
Hâlî lahû ka'amali wa niyyatî

I have made my Lord, my King, my Master, the Owner of all my entirety, my states, my deeds, and intentions are His

رددت بالله وبالرّسول
من خالفوا حقًّا ونلت سؤلي

Raddata billâhi wa bir rassûli
Man khâlaful haqqa wa niltu suli

I have repelled by Allah and the Apostle, those who oppose the truth. And, I obtained requirements.

برّأني الإله من شرك ومن
كلّ نفاق وسعادتّي ضمن

Barra anil illâhu min chirkin wa min
Kulli nifaaqine wa sahâdâtî damîn

Allah has freed me from all association and hypocrisy and ensured my entry into Paradise

برّأني من عيب نفسي بالنّبي
صلّي عليه بسلام مطنب

Bara'anî mine 'aybi nafsî bi-nabi
Sallâ 'Alayhi bissalâmin mutnibi

Allah has exemplified me from the vices of my soul through the Prophet, may an endless blessing and salvation be bestowed upon him

هو اللّذي لم أري غيره
ولا أراه في شيء هدا ونوّلا

**Huwal lazī lam ara ghayrahû walâ
Arahû fî chay-in hadâ wa nawwalâ**

I do not see anything other than him and I
I will not let myself be guided or possessed by anything else

محمّد صلّي عليه بسلام
وسيلتي له ولي قاد الكلام

**Muhammadun sallâ'alayi bi salam
Wassîlatî lahû wali gâdal kalâm**

Muhammad, blessings and salutations be upon him, is the rope that binds me to Him. And He has granted me eloquence

فرّحني الأكرم تفريحا يدوم
بأنّني خلّ وحبّ وخديم

**Farrahanîl akramu tafrîkhan yadûm
Bi annanî khîlun wa khîbbun wa khadim**

The Most Generous has granted me lasting joy, that I am a friend, an intimate, and a servant

له خطابي ومحا الأكدارا
ولسوانا وجّه الغدّارا

**Lahû khitâbî wa mahal akdârâ
Wa lisiwânâ wajahal 'ghaadârâ**

This speech is addressed to Him. And He has dispelled my troubles and has directed the great deceiver to others

أيّدتنا علي العدي فغلبوا
ولسوانا صاغرين انقلبوا

Ayyadtana alal 'idâ faghulibū
Wa lisiwânâ saghirinâ-n qalabū

He has helped me against the enemies,
And they were defeated and turned back to others

تسليم باق قاد لي ثوابا
علي اللّذي أورثني ثوابا

Taslimu bâqin qâda issawâbâ
Ala lazī awrassanî thawâbâ

May peace of the Ever-Lasting be upon him (Muhammad – pbuh) who made me inherit the rewards

علي اللّذي طلب كوني الخديم
له سلاما ذي البريّة الخديم

Alllazî Talabani kawniyal khadim
Lahû saláma zil bariyyatil xadim

Upon him who requested that I am his servant (Muhammad) be the blessing and salvation of the Lord, Master of Mankind

لمن له كلّيتي عباده
حمدي ومن خالفني أباده

Liman lahû kulliyatî 'ibadah
Hamdi wa man khâlafani abâdah

My praises are dedicated to whom I submit my entirety, my worship, [and] who destroys whoever contradicts me

ملك الّذي ليس له مباه
لي قاد ما غاب عن المباه

Mulkul-lazee laytha lahû mubâhi
Lee khâda maå ghâba anil mubahi

The dominion of Him who has no equal has brought for me unseen graces

ناجاني العليم والخبير
وكان لي الواسع والكبير

Nâjaaniyal 'alîmu wal khabiru
Wa jâdalil wâssi'u wal kabîru

The All-Knowing and All-Aware has communicated with me
The All-Embracing and the Greatest benefited me

فرّحني الجميل نعم النّافع
أعلاني الملك زهو الرّافع

Farrahanîl jamílu Nihman- nâfihu
A'lâniyal maliku wah- war-râfihu

The All-Beautiful made me glad, exalted be the Most Beneficial
The Ruler (King) lifted my rank, He is the Exalted

ساق مكارهي لمن قبل نحا
مضرّتي من لي يقود المنحا

Sâqa makârihî liman qablu
Nahâ, Madarratî man lî yaqudu minha

He who inundated me with graces has turned me against my former persecutors.

ملّكني الملك والمليك
والمالك اللّذي له تمليك

Malakanî maliku wal-malīkū
Wal māliku lazī lahû tamliku

The King, who bestows an abundance and owns everything has imparted me

أجرا كبيرا وثوابا وجزا
والوعد لي في رمضان نجزا

Ajran kabiran wa thawaban wa jazza
Wal wa'duli fi ramadâna najază

A huge salary and a very great reward. The compensation and the promise came to me in the month of Ramadan.

أجر اللّذي ما عنده لا ينفد
وصل لي ومااعترّاه نفد

Ajrul lazî mâhindahu lâ yanfadu
Wasala lî wama'tarahu nafadu

The salary of the One who holds that which is inexhaustible has come to me and his wages will not be exhausted.

خدمة خير العالمين أحمدا
عليه تسليما كريم حمّدا

Khidmatu khayril âlaminâ Ahmadâ
Alayhi taslimâ karîmin humida

My service to the best of mankind in the universe, Ahmad.
Allah, the Generous, worthy of praise grants him blessing and salvation

فرّحت القلب ونفسي طيّبت
وبمكارهي لغيري ذهبت

Farrahatil qalba wa nafsî tay'yabat
Wa bimakânihî lighayri dhahabat

Has brought joy to my heart and sweetness to my soul and has taken away my persecutions to others.

يسرّ خير العالمين قلمي
عليه تسليما مزيل الألم

Yasuru khayral ālamīna qalami
Alayhi taslimâ muzilil alami

My pen has delighted the best being of the universe, on him be blessing and salvation, that has put an end to my suffering.

للمصطفي وجّهت ما لي قادا
نفعا بلا مضرّة فانقادا

Lî Mustafâ wajjahtu mâ lî gâdâ
Nafhan Bila mandarin fanqaada

To the Chosen One, I have directed all that has come of use and without harm. And that which is useful has shown itself docile.

هو الشّفيع وهو الشّجاع
به محا ظلمي والأوجاع

Huwa chafi'u wa huwa- chuja'u
Bihî Maha zulmiya wall awjâ'u

He is the intercessor. And he is the courageous one. Thanks to him my persecutions and sufferings have ceased

مـحّمد صلّي عليه الله
في الآل والصّحب ومن والاه

Muhammadun sallâ Alayhi lâhu
Fil âli wa sahib waman wâlâhu

Muhammad may Allah's blessing be upon his family, his companions, and anyone who is attached to him.

محا بلائي ومحا أمراضي
وبالرّضي تنقاد لي أغراضي

Mahâ balâ-i wa mahâ amrâdi
Wa bir ridâ tanqanadu lî aghrâdî

He has made my trials disappear, ceased my illnesses, and with approval, all my wishes are fulfilled.

نبيّنا المختار خير الأنبيا
عليه تسليما حبيبي ربّيا

Nabiyyunâl Mukhtaru Khair ul anbiya
Alayhi taslimâ Habibi rabbiyâ

Our Prophet, the Chosen One, is the best of the Prophets, may the blessing and salvation of my Friend, my Lord, be upon him.

قدّت له كلّيتي في العلن
والسّرّ وهو لي قاد ولن

Qudtu lahû kulliyatî fil "Alani
Was cirri Wahwa Liya qâda walani

I have surrendered to Him my everything inwardly and outwardly, and He has given me (walane)[2]

---

[2] Walane is a reference to the Quranic Ayah (walan yajhala laahu lil kafeerīna alal mūmineena sabīlane)

رفعت خدمتي إلي الوسيلة
صلّي عليه من أري تفضيله

Rafahtu qidmati ilal wassilah
Sallâ 'Alayhi man arâ tafdîlah

I have offered my services to my intercessor. May he be blessed by the One who has made him superior.

رفعت خدمتي إلي الماحي السند
ولسوانا ساق كلّ من فند

Rafah khidmatî ill Mahi sanad
Wa lisiwânā sâga kulla man fanad

I have offered my services to the Wiper of Sins, He who drove away from us all deniers

هو النّبي والرّسول والخليل
وهو الحبيب ويكثّر الخليل

Huwa Nabiyyu war Rassûlu wal Khalil
Wahl hábību wa yukathirul xalil

He is the Prophet, the Messenger, the Friend. And he is the Intimate and he multiplies the little.

تسليم باق لا يزال سندا
علي النّبي والرّسول أحمدا

Taslimu bâqin lâ yazālu thanada
Alan Nabiyyi war- rassûli Ahmada

May the salvation of the Eternal One who will never cease to be, be upon the Prophet, the Messenger Ahmad

أبقِي سلامي الكريم الصّمد
علي النّبي وسيلتي محمّد

Abqâ salâmayil karîmi Samadi
Alan Nabi wasîlati Muhammadi

May the Generous, the Eternal send
blessing and salvation on the Prophet, my intercessor Muhammad.

علي النّبي وسيلتي محمّد
أبقِي سلامي الكريم الصّمد

Alan Nabî wasaílatî Muhammadi
Abqa salamayyil karîmi thammadi

May the most lasting blessing and salvation come through the care of
the Generous, the Eternal, to my intercessor Muhammad

يا الله يا قادر يا مقتدر
يا من إليه جوده يبتدر

Yal lâhu yâ qâdiru yâ muqtadiru
Yâ man ilayya jûduhû yabtadiru

Oh my Lord! Oh the Almighty! Oh the Able!
You whose bounty has been poured out upon me.

ناجيتك اليوم وقبل اليوم
ولي جعلت الفطر فوق صوم

Nājaytukal yawma wa qablal yawmi
Wali ja'altal fitra fawqas-sawmi

I address this speech to You alone on this day and before this day. You
have made my Iftār prevail over my observance of fasting

جأت بذا القصيد شاكرا لكا
به وقبل لي قدّت فضلكا

Jitu bi dhal qasîdi châkiran lakâ
Bihî wa qablu liya qudta fadlaka

I come to You with this poem to thank You because, before this day, You have already granted me superiority.

زنت قصيدتي ته شكورا
ولم تزل يا مالكي شكورا

Zintu qasîdatî tihi chukurâ
Walam tazal yâ mâlikî chakûrâ

I have embellished this ode as a token of gratitude which, Oh my Master, I will never cease to proclaim my gratitude.

أكرمتني إكرام من ما شا فعل
وكل ما أردته منك انفعل

Akramtani ikramaman ma cha fahal
Wa Kullu ma aradtuhū mikan infa'al

You have bestowed upon me the honors of the One who does what he wants. And all that I want to accomplish becomes feasible because of You.

أعطيتني يا ربّ من لدنكا
ذكرا حكيما فرضيت عنكا

Ataytani yà Rabi min ladunka
Zikrane hakîman faradītu Anka

O, my Lord, You have brought to me a Holy Book from You and I am Grateful to You

باركت لي يا ربّ في حروفي
وغيرها وجدّت بالمعروف

Barakta li yaa Rabbi fi hurūfi
Wa ghayrihâ wa judta bil marūfi

Oh Master! You have blessed my writings and other possessions and
You have shown me unlimited generosity.

ملّكتني بكونك الكريما
ما قاد لي التّبشير والتّكريما

Mal-laktani bi kawnikal kareemaâ
Ma khada li-tabchira wa takreema

Through your generosity You imparted
me abundant favors and high regard.

أعطيتني ما القلب أنسا كلّما
مضي من الضّر محوت الظّلما

Ahtaytanî ma-l qalba ansa Kullamâ
Madhamina-d-durri, mahawta zulamâ

You bestowed upon me that which made me forget my ordeals
You removed all injustice done to me.

كافئني من ما له كفوًا أحد
بما لغيري سا ق كلّ من جحد

Kâfaanî man ma lahû kufan ahad
Bimâ lighayri sâqa Kulla man jihad

He who has no equal has rewarded me
in a way that drove away from me, towards others, every negator.

أكرمني بقل هو الله أحد
ربّي ولم يكن له كفوًا أحد

**Akramanî bi qul huwal lâhu ahad
Rabbî wa lam yakun lahû kufan ahad**

My Lord has granted me graces through (Ikhlas) and no one is equal to Him.

ناجاني الله المكرّم الصّمد
تناجيا به كفاني الكمد

**Nâjâniyal lahûl mukarrimu Samad
Tanadjiyane bihî kafaniyal kama**

Allah, who honors and is the Eternal One, has granted me a conversion that has removed my tiredness

وجّه لي الأكرم أنفع الكرم
وضرري بغير ردّ لي انصرم

**Wajjaha lîl akramu anfa'al Karam
Wa dararī bighayri Radin lin saram**

The most Generous granted me the most useful marks of generosity. My persecutions are gone in a hurry.

أسأله كون تهو القصيدة
خارقة لعادة مفيدة

**As-aluhu (Kawna) tihi-l qassîda
(Khaarikhatane) lihaadatine mufîda**

I implored Him (Allah) so that this poem might be beneficial and outstanding.

ياحيّ يا قيّوم صلّ بسلام
علي اللّذي جاء بأحسن كلام

Yâ hayyû ya qayyûmu Salli bi salam
"All lazy ja-a bi ahsani kalam

Oh Ever-Living One! Oh Lord, grant blessing and salvation to the one who brings the most charming speech

علي اللّذي جاء بأحسن الكلام
صلّ وسلّم والتقبّل ذا الكلام

Ala lazî jâa bi Hassani kalam
Salli wa Salim wal taqabbal Zal kalam

To the one who brings the most charming speech, grant blessings, and greetings.

منّ علي قارء ذي الحروف
بما يفوق الظّنّ من معروف

Munna 'alâ qari-i zil hurûfi
Bima yafūquz Zanna min ma'rûfi

Grant to anyone who reads this poem a gift beyond what they can imagine.

لناظم الحروف خلّد الرّباح
يا من كفاه ذا الغرور والنّباح

Li nâzimil hurufi khalidir rabâh
Yâ man kafâhu Zal ghurûri wan nubâh

For the one who composed it, make the benefit last, O You who protected it against the men of illusions (the colonialist) and [their] barking dogs.

ولِيّ يا رحمان يا رحيم يا
حيّ ويا قيّوم يامكرم يا

**Walyyu yâ rahmânu yâ rahîmu yâ
Hayyu wa yâ qayyûmu yâ mukrimiya**

Oh Friend! Oh Clement! Oh Merciful!
Oh Living! Ô Eternal One! O Generous One!

ناجاك عبدك الخديم ذا صلاة
مسلّما علي مزحزح القلاة

**Nâjâka abdukal khadimu zâ salâh
Musalimane alâ muzahzihil qulah**

Your servant has just communicated with You (through this qasīda),
while praying upon the One who repelled the haters.

**SUBHÂNA RABBIKA RABBIL IZZATI HAM-MAA YASIFUN WA SALAMU
ALAL MURSALINA WAL HAMDU LIL LAAHI RABBI IL ALAMIN**

GLORY AND PURITY TO OUR LORD, THE MASTER OF POWER AND
CONSIDERATION, FAR ABOVE THE DESCRIPTIONS THEY INVENT.
PEACE AND SALVATION TO THE MESSENGERS. AND PRAISE IS TO GOD,
THE LORD, AND MASTER OF THE UNIVERSE.

CONSIDERATION FOR WA KĀANA HÀQQAN

Serigne Bassirou Mbacke and Wa Kāana Hàqqan

Serigne Bassirou Mbacké is said to have had a lot of regard and considerations for Wa Kāana Hàqqan.

Serigne Abdu Hadr Mbacke and Wa Kāana Hàqqan

It has been said, when a talibé came to Serigne Abdu Hadr Mbacké, He used to ask them, "Baa Wa Kaana Ngua", a way of saying or asking, "Did you read Wa Kāana Hàqqan?" He urged the talibés to admire this qasīda.

Serigne Fallou Mbacké and Wa Kāana Hàqqan:

Serigne Modou Bousso Dieng, son of Serigne Fallou Mbacké who recounted these facts, that there was a period during which Serigne Fallou lived difficult times. He went to explain to Serigne Touba his situation. Serigne Touba observed him for a few moments before giving him the qasīda Wa Kāana Hàqqan. Serigne Fallou remained attached to it, "Since then I have nothing more to complain about", he would say later.

Serigne Saliou Mbacke and Wa Kāana Hàqqan:

A Dahira from Italy came to Serigne Saliou to accomplish their Ziar, at the end of the discussions the guide recommends them to "read this qasīda every day". So he recommended it to everyone, especially the talibé Mourides.

Everyone that had at some time, been close to Serigne Saliou Mbacké can witness or tell a story about Serigne Saliou and Wa Kāana Hàqqan. Also, everyone knows that He was reading the qasīda daily.

Extracted from an article by Siidy Muhammad

ABOUT THE AUTHOR

Shaykh Mbacke Gueye was born on April 10, 1979, to Massamba Gueye and Aissatu Diop. He is affiliated with the Baye Fall Community of Mame Shaykh Ibrahima Fall. Shaykh Gueye is a talibé of Serigne Abdoulaye Fall, Borom Ndar Fall. This translation into English with transliteration is among his projects to expand and disseminate the works of Shaykh Ahmadou Bamba, affectionately known as Khadim Rasoul, to the world. He has degrees in both Arabic and English; he also speaks French. His contributions to the Mouride Community include lectures on Shaykh Ahmadou Bamba, Shaykh Ibrahima Fall, and other great disciples (talibé) to invigorate the present generation to follow their examples.

Mbacke Gueye
May Allah grant him Afiyah and Khewel...
by the blessings of Cheikh Ibrahima Fall

Printed in Great Britain
by Amazon